DATE DUE

JY 21 '93			
NO 16 '93			
DE 20 '93			
JA 22 '94			
FE 5 '94			
AP 21 '94			
OC 18 '94			
NO 15 '94			
JE 15 '95			
FE 8 96			
SE 12			
OC 1 96			
MY24 '99			
JA 19 '05			

DEMCO 38-297

i Wonder

What A Rainforest Is

· · · · · · · · · · · · ·

plants

i Wonder
What A Rainforest Is

· · · · · · · · · · · · · ·
nd other facts about plants

Annabelle Donati
ustrated by Sharron O'Neil

A GOLDEN BOOK • NEW YORK
Western Publishing Company, Inc., Racine, Wisconsin 53404

Produced by Graymont Enterprises, Inc., Norfolk, Connecticut
Producer: *Ruth Lerner Perle*
Design: *Michele Italiano-Perla*
Editorial consultant: *Mary Ann McGourty*, Hillside Garden Nursery, Norfolk, Connectiut

ISBN: 0-307-11322-1/ISBN: 0-307-61322-4 (lib. bdg.)   A   MCMXCII

Contents

What does it take to be a plant?

Plants can't walk or swim from place to place as other living things can. They can't speak, or sing, or roar. But plants can do something that no other living thing can do: They make their own food. Plants need only sun, water, and air, and most also need soil.

Even though plants are different from one another, there are some things that are the same about most of them:

Seeds and flowers

Flowering plants make seeds that can grow into new plants.

Leaves

Leaves are food-making factories that use sunlight as their source of energy. Leaves contain a green substance called *chlorophyll*. Inside the leaves, the chlorophyll is mixed with water taken from the roots and with a gas called *carbon dioxide*, which the leaves take from the air. This mixture makes a kind of sugar that the plant stores. This process is called *photosynthesis*.

Stems

Flowers and their leaves have soft, fleshy stems that keep them standing upright. These stems die in the fall and sprout again in the spring. Trees, shrubs, and bushes have strong, woody stems that last the plant's lifetime.

Roots

Most plants are anchored to the ground by their roots, which grow down into the soil. Roots collect water and other nutrients from the soil and send them up through the stems to the rest of the plant.

Is a fern a plant?

Yes. Ferns, mosses, and other simple plants don't have flowers, but they do manufacture their own food.

Is a quartz rock a plant?

No. Some rock crystals look just like flowers, but they are minerals. They cannot reproduce themselves, and they don't make their own food.

Is a sea anemone a plant?

No. Sea anemones and some sponges look just like water plants, but they must capture their food. This makes them animals.

Tell Me More

The Indian pipe, or ghost flower, has no chlorophyll. Like the mushroom, it gets its nourishment from rotting wood and leaves. But it makes seeds like a true flower.

Amazing but TRUE

Some plants, like the Venus flytrap, make their own food but also catch and eat insects. When a fly or other insect touches its sticky open leaves, the leaves snap shut and it digests its catch.

Why are flowers so fancy?

Their perfume wafts through the air, and they are a joy to see. In fact, no other living things come in as many shapes and bright colors as flowers. But nature has a special reason for making flowers look the way they do.

A flower's main job is to make seeds so that new plants will grow. To make seeds, flowers must be *pollinated*. That means the pollen from one flower must, in most cases, reach another flower of the same kind. Since flowers can't move from place to place, they depend on moving things in nature to help them. The way a flower looks and smells is one way of making sure it will be pollinated.

How do flowers get pollinated?

Bees, birds, butterflies, and bats are attracted by the color, shape, or sweet perfume of flowers. But that's not all. At the center of most blossoms is a tiny cup that holds a sweet liquid called *nectar*. All these creatures love to sip nectar.

As they reach inside the flower to get the nectar, some of the powdery pollen gets stuck on their feet, backs, and bellies. When they fly to get nectar from another flower of the same kind, the pollen on their bodies rubs off on that flower, and a seed begins to form.

The carrion flower plant has blossoms with drab-colored petals that look like raw meat. These blossoms have a meatlike odor that attracts the flies that pollinate them.

Why are flowers differently colored?

Each kind of flower is designed to attract different kinds of pollinators.

Flowers that attract bees are usually blue, purple, yellow, or white—the colors a bee sees best.

Flowers that attract moths are usually white or yellow so that moths can see them in the dark.

Flowers that attract birds and butterflies are usually red or orange, since birds and butterflies like bright colors.

How does a seed become a plant?

All living things in nature reproduce themselves. Mammals have eggs inside their bodies that grow into baby animals. Birds lay eggs that hatch into baby chicks. Plants don't have eggs, but they have something that works in the same way—seeds.

What is a seed?

A seed is a plant that has not started to grow. Each seed is a complete package containing a tiny plant and enough food to get it started in life. Every plant has a different kind of seed. Seeds come in a variety of shapes and sizes. Peas and lima beans are seeds, and so are the kernels of corn. Some coconuts are the biggest seeds.

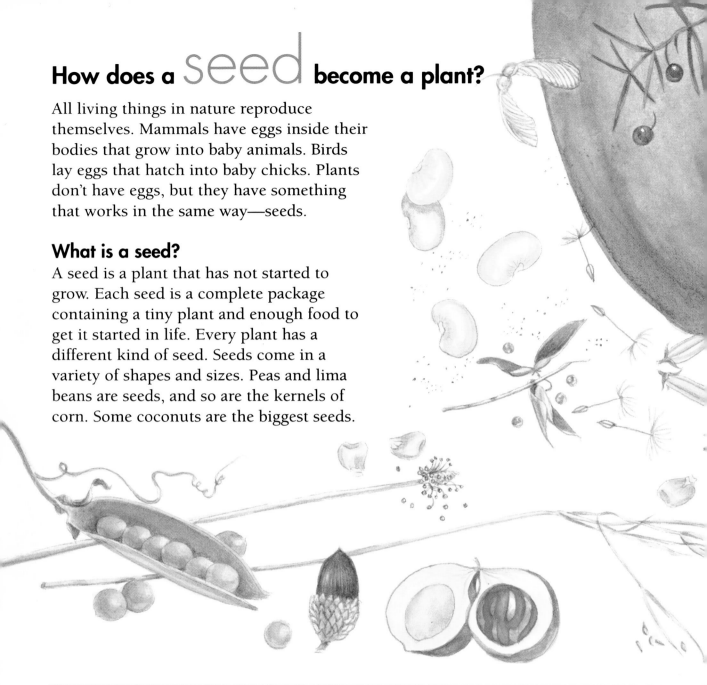

How do seeds sprout?

1. When a seed is planted and watered, its protective seed coat is soaked off.
2. The seed is now ready to sprout.
3. It forms roots that push down into the earth to collect water.
4. The leaves and stem push up through the soil and reach toward the sun and air.
5. The young plant is called a *seedling*.

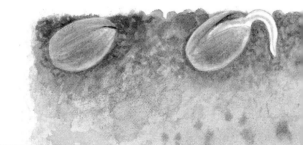

Do all plants have seeds?

No. Ferns and some other simple plants have *spores* instead of seeds. Spores look like tiny brown specks. Round clumps of them are seen on the underside of the fern leaf. When spores fall on the ground, they grow into new ferns.

Amazing
but TRUE

Coconut seeds have a waterproof shell designed to float in water. The milk inside the coconut provides the liquid the seed needs to sprout when it washes up on a sandy beach.

How do blossoms make seeds?

Most blossoms have both male and female parts. The male part is called a *stamen*. It is a tiny stalk with a little sack at the end of it called an *anther*. The anther contains a powder called *pollen*.

The female part is called a *pistil*. It is a long tube and looks like a tiny straw at the center of the flower. At the top of the tube is a sticky substance that catches the pollen. At the bottom of the tube is a larger part called the *ovary*.

When a pollen grain gets stuck on the pistil, it forms a pollen tube. The tube grows down to the ovary and joins one of the egg cells there. When the egg cell unites with the pollen, it forms the tiny *embryo* plant that becomes a seed.

Amazing but TRUE

An apple is the ovary that was once at the center of a tiny apple blossom. The seeds inside the apple are the egg cells that united with the pollen.

pistil

anther with pollen

stamen

ovary with seeds

pistil

10

Why can't a peanut make up its mind?

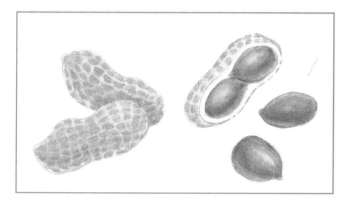

Because it has no choice. When the peanut seed sprouts, the plant and flower grow straight up toward the sun like most other plants. After its yellow blossom has been pollinated, the petals fall off and the seed pod, or shell, begins to form.

Then the strangest thing happens. When the seeds are about to ripen, the weight of the seed pods makes the stalks bend down toward the earth, and the pods bury themselves in the ground. In that way, the peanut plant plants its own seeds.

Do you dig for peanuts?

Yes, indeed, you do! When peanuts are harvested, they are dug out of the ground like potatoes.

Is a peanut a pea or a nut?

A peanut is neither a pea nor a nut. It is a member of the pea and bean family of vegetables called *legumes*. The shape of its shell is similar to that of a pea pod, and the nuts inside the shell are similar to the peas inside the pod.

Amazing but TRUE

Peanuts are delicious and nutritious eaten plain. They are also used to make foods such as peanut oil, peanut butter, and a kind of coffee. They have even been used to make soap! George Washington Carver, an agricultural researcher, invented many different uses for the peanut.

11

What's the reason for a tree?

Trees are beautiful. That alone seems enough reason for their being. But beauty is not all they give to the earth. Their leaves give us shade. Their roots keep the soil in place so that wind and water can't wash it away. Their branches produce fruits, nuts, and flowers. Animals depend on trees for shelter and food. Trees add oxygen and moisture to the air we breathe and help reduce air pollution by using up poisonous gas called carbon dioxide.

What makes a plant a tree?

Its trunk. Trees have tall, round wood trunks, most of which grow thicker each year.

What are tree rings?

When a tree trunk is cut across, you can see a pattern that looks like rings. Each ring tells how much the tree has grown in a year. Add up the rings and you'll know how old the tree is.

Tell Me More

There are three types of trees:

Broadleaf trees, like maple, oak, and apple, have flat leaves growing from spreading woody branches. These trees shed their leaves in autumn.

Conifer trees, like spruce and pine, have leaves that look like needles. They are green year round.

Palm trees don't have branches. Their huge leaves grow out of the trunk.

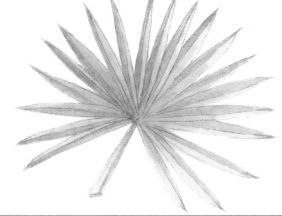

Why do some trees look different each season?

Conifer trees and palm trees are green year round, but broadleaf trees, like this chestnut, change with each season.

In winter, the chestnut tree's branches are bare. The tree is resting.

In spring, the tree's sap, or juice, starts to run through the trunk and branches. New leaves appear on the branches. Chlorophyll gives the leaves their green color. Soon blossoms appear. When the blossoms are pollinated, seeds start to form.

In summer, the leaves grow larger and become a deeper green. They manufacture lots of nourishment for the tree and the growing seeds.

In autumn, the chlorophyll has done its work and disappears. Now we see the real color of the leaves: red, orange, yellow, or purple. Now the seeds are fully grown and fall to the ground. As the weather gets colder, the sap stops flowing into the leaves. They dry up and fall off.

Why does poison ivy itch?

Plants have different ways of protecting themselves from being eaten by animals. Roses have thorns, thistles have barbs, cacti have spines. Some plants protect themselves by releasing a poison. Poison ivy is one of the more common of these. The whole plant, including the roots, contains a kind of oil. When you touch any part of the plant, it releases the oil, which makes most people's skin break out in a blistering, itchy rash.

What does poison ivy look like?

Poison ivy has shiny green leaves that grow in sprigs of three leaflets and look as if they had just been polished. In the fall, the leaves turn a reddish green, and little white berries grow around the stem.

Amazing but TRUE

Even the smoke from burning poison ivy is poisonous. The fumes can cause loss of breath and coughing.

Where does poison ivy grow?

Poison ivy grows in sun or shade. It can be found in the woods or on the beach. It can grow bunched together like a shrub. It can climb up a tree or creep along a wall.

Is it safe to touch poison ivy in winter?

No. Poison ivy causes a rash year round.

Do animals get poison ivy?

Only human beings seem to be allergic to poison ivy. Birds love its berries.

Tell Me More

There are other plants, including poison sumac and poison oak, with leaves that cause rashes.

One of the most dangerous plants is the tobacco plant. Its leaves don't cause a rash, but when tobacco is smoked, poisons that can cause several deadly diseases, including cancer and heart disease, collect in the body.

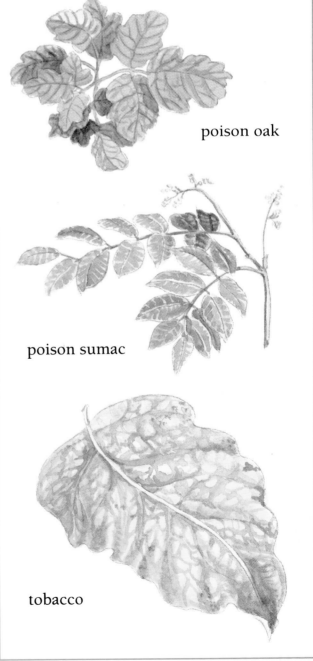

poison oak

poison sumac

tobacco

17

How does the pit get in the peach?

When peaches—or any other fruit—ripen, animals are attracted by their smell and bright colors. They come to eat the soft, fleshy part of the fruit, but they don't enjoy the hard, rough pit. This is all part of nature's plan. The pit is not supposed to be eaten. It is a seed, and it is meant to grow into another peach tree.

Here's how the pit gets in the peach:

1 In the spring, the peach tree has beautiful, perfumed blossoms on its branches. The wind and insects pollinate the blossoms so they will form seeds.

2 The petals and stamens fall off, leaving small round green knobs. The inside of each knob will be the seed, or pit. The outside will be the thick coat that protects the seed. This is the part that will be eaten.

3 The green knobs grow and grow. The little peaches are not yet ripe. They are still hard and sour.

4 Soon the fleshy outer covering ripens. It is yellowish pink, velvety soft, and juicy. The fruit looks and smells delicious. Animals and birds come to see and taste.

5 Some peaches are carried away by animals that eat the fruit. They drop the pits on the ground. Some of these pits may be pushed into the soil. Then, if they get enough water and warmth, they will sprout and new peach trees will start to grow.

Do potatoes really have eyes?

Potatoes are swellings, or *tubers*, on the roots of potato plants where an extra supply of food (starch and sugar) is stored. The bumps on the outside of a potato may look like small closed eyes, but they can't see or blink. The eyes are really little buds of plants, ready to sprout.

Because a potato has so much plant food in it, the buds sometimes start to sprout even without being planted. Then the potato becomes soft and wrinkled because the new plants are feeding on the stored starch.

How do potatoes grow?

Although potatoes may be grown from seeds, a faster way is to plant the buds. The potato is cut up so that each piece has an eye on it. When the cutting is planted, it sends stems and leaves above the ground and roots down into the soil. Some of the roots swell and make new potatoes.

Amazing *but* TRUE

Begonias, African violets, jade plants, and many other plants can make new plants from pieces of their own leaves.

Bulbs

Another way of planting without seeds is to use bulbs. As with potatoes, bulbs are little plant buds that contain lots of nourishment for the sprouting plant.

When bulbs are planted, they develop roots, stems, and leaves. Some plants, such as tulips, lilies, daffodils, onions, and garlic, are grown from bulbs.

21

Where do raisins grow?

There's no such thing as a raisin plant, even though raisins are fruits. That's because raisins are really dried grapes. Other fruits, such as dates, plums, apricots, figs, and peaches, may also be eaten dry. Dried fruits look wrinkled and shriveled, but they are delicious and make a healthful snack.

How do grapes grow?

Grapes don't grow on bushes or on trees. The grape plant has special stems called vines. Vines are slender, bendable stems that can climb. Little clinging roots grow out of these stems and attach themselves to poles, walls, or other supports. Grapevines climb with the help of special short, curly stems called *tendrils*. The grape plant has small flowers that grow in tight clusters. These develop into shiny bunches of green, black, or red grapes.

Tell Me More

After they are picked, some grapes are dried and made into raisins. Some are cooked with sugar and made into jam. Some are squeezed and made into juice. Some are fermented and made into wine. Of course, some are just eaten fresh off the stem.

How are fruits dried?

For fruits to dry, their water or juice must be removed. They may be spread out in the sun to dry, or processed by special machines that remove their liquid. Dried fruits don't need to be refrigerated.

Amazing *but* TRUE

If you soak raisins or other dried fruits in water for a few hours, they will regain their original shape.

Where does maple syrup come from?

In the spring, the sap starts running freely inside most trees. It runs up through the trunk and into the branches. The sugar maple's sap is very special. It has so much sugar in it that it can be made into a delicious syrup—maple syrup. If some of the sap is removed, the tree can survive. But if too much is taken, there is not enough to nourish the tree and it dies.

How do we get syrup from the tree?

1. In order to get at the sap, a hollow tube is pushed through the bark of the tree to where the sap is flowing.

2. A small bucket is hung at the opening of the tube to collect the sap.

3. The sap is boiled long enough to remove most of the water. What remains is the delicious sweet syrup, ready to pour on pancakes.

Tell Me More

Maple syrup isn't the only thing we get from tree sap. Rubber is made from a milky sap called *latex*. The bark of the rubber tree is slit, and the sap is drained into containers. Fresh cuts are made every day or two.

The sapodilla tree's latex produces *chicle*, the main ingredient in chewing gum.

Amazing but TRUE

Animals have hearts that pump their blood and make it circulate through the body. Sap can run up through a tree trunk and into the branches and leaves against the pull of gravity—all without the help of a pump. Scientists don't agree about how this works.

How can water plants float?

Most plants grow on land. Some, like cat-tails and watercress, grow at the water's edge. But there are some plants that actually live right in the water. These plants have special ways of staying afloat.

The most spectacular of the water plants are water lilies and lotuses. Their flat round leaves, which resemble little rafts, float easily on the surface of the water. And their stems have tiny air spaces that act like inflated life vests, keeping them from sinking.

The waxy flowers have a beautiful range of colors: shades of pink, yellow, white, lavender, and green. They lie gracefully on the surface of the water, opening their petals in the morning and closing them in the evening.

Do water lilies have roots?

Yes. Their roots reach down and anchor the plant at the bottom of the water, and their long swaying stems reach up to the surface of the water to support the blossom and bring it nourishment.

Amazing but TRUE

Water lilies that grow in the Amazon rainforest in South America have leaves six feet wide—larger than most dinner-table tops—and flowers three feet across.

Tell Me More

Lotus blossoms were considered sacred in ancient China. That's why so many Chinese antiques have lotus blossom designs.

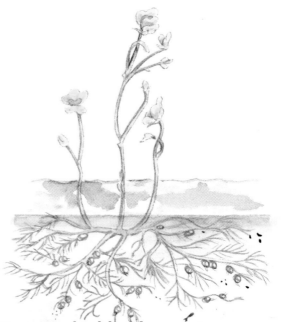

Beware the bladderwort!

The bladderwort plant has underwater leaves that have little hollow *bladders*, or air sacs, to keep them afloat. But that's not all the bladders do. Each bladder has a tiny opening that works like a trapdoor. When a water insect or tiny fish swims by, the bladder sucks it in through the opening. Then the opening closes tight and the victim is caught inside.

Why does the bladderwort catch fish and insects?

The bladderwort makes its own food through photosynthesis, but it also needs special nutrients that it can get only from meat.

How can a cactus live with so little water?

Cactus plants are designed to live in hot, dry, sandy places. Their roots are close to the surface so they can catch every drop of rain. When it rains, the cactus stores the water in the spongy or hollow tissues of its stems. Many cacti can expand and contract depending on how much water they have. The skin of a cactus is thick and waxy. This prevents loss of water.

Why doesn't a cactus have leaves?

Instead of leaves, most cacti have needlelike spines that protect them from thirsty animals that want to get at the water in their stems.

The giant saguaro

The saguaro is the largest of all cacti. Some grow to be fifty feet tall. That's taller than a five-story building. But saguaros are not considered trees, because they don't have a woody bark. Nevertheless, woodpeckers build nests inside their stems.

Do cacti have flowers?

Cacti have large beautiful flowers. Some bloom only at night. Some bloom for just a day or two. Some bloom only once every few years.

A large saguaro cactus can hold ten tons of water. That's about as much as sixty bathtubs full of water.

What is a
rainforest?

A rainforest is a huge and wonderful jungle—a tangle of giant trees and flowers growing in hot and steamy tropical regions of the earth. It is home to thousands of different jungle animals, birds, and plants. One of the largest rainforests is the Amazon jungle in South America.

Why is the rainforest so dark?

The leaves of the trees are so dense that they form a kind of shade umbrella, or *canopy*, over the forest. Very little sunlight shines through, so the forest floor is always dark.

Life in the treetops

Much of jungle life takes place in the high branches. Brightly feathered birds blend in with colorful flowers and fruits. Monkeys swing from tree to tree on thick vines called *lianas*. Snakes curl around the limbs of trees, and sloths hang from them. Even some of the jungle cats find safety in the branches.

Why are rainforests important?

Rainforests help to keep the earth's air moist and clean. Their plants and trees give us medicines that cure many diseases. If the trees continue to be cut down, most of the wild animals and plants inhabiting the rainforests will have no other place to live. They will disappear from the earth forever.

The largest flower on earth grows in a rainforest—it is the rafflesia. This flower can be nearly three feet wide and weigh fifteen pounds!

Tell Me More

Though you have come to the last page of this book, you are only beginning to know about the wonderful true-life stories of plants. Scientists who study plants are called *botanists*. But you don't have to be a botanist to enjoy finding out more about the amazing plant kingdom.

There seems to be a plan and a purpose for everything in nature. Large or small, beautiful or strange, each plant and animal has a role to fulfill. Each has an effect on something else that sooner or later has an effect on us.

Here are some more amazing-but-true facts about plants to start you on your way to new discoveries:

- The leafy canopy covering the rainforest floor is so dense that it can take hours—sometimes days—before the rain hits the ground.

- Ten-thousand-year-old arctic lupine seeds were found frozen and buried in northern Canada. To everyone's amazement, these ancient seeds sprouted just a few days after they were planted.

- Some mushrooms give off a strange green, orange, or white light.

- When an insect falls into the Asian pitcher plant's pitcher-shaped flower, a special liquid in the flower digests the insect.

- Trees are the largest living things on earth. Some are even bigger than whales. The heaviest tree of all is the giant sequoia. It can weigh two million pounds. The tallest tree is the California redwood, which grows as high as four hundred feet. That's four times the length of a giant blue whale.

INDEX

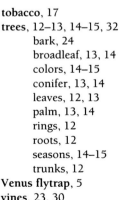